WIFE SCHOOL

Using God's Word to build a stronger marriage

Lisa Ellis Williams

Marriage requires continuing education!

Lisa!

ISBN-13: 978-1484815977
ISBN-10: 1484815971

Dedication

This study is dedicated to my Heavenly Father who has proven Himself to be real, steadfast, and true in my life. He has drawn me with loving kindness out of a love based on feelings alone and into an everlasting love. My heart is eternally grateful and my response is to accept this assignment and teach you the lessons I have learned in my personal "Wife School" experience. May your love life be blessed exceedingly and abundantly more than all you could ask or think.
-*Lisa Ellis Williams*

Acknowledgments

I must take a moment and offer a huge thank you to the people who have been faithful in prayer, and lovingly supported me as I developed this message. Their names are Stuart Williams, Rachel Williams, Hailey Williams, Gavin Williams, Reginald Dixon, Lori Dixon, DeLonda Adams, Jill Hart, Krissah Williams-Thompson, Calvin Nophlin, Barbara Nophlin and the Wives On Purpose. I love you all. Without your friendship and constant encouragement, I would never have finished this project. You are the wind beneath my wings!

About the Author

Lisa Ellis Williams affectionately calls her journey *"wife school."* It is her testimony of tests passed and lessons learned after living through seven years of separation, divorce and ultimate remarriage (to the same husband).

Lisa began a career in public health education and wellness teaching men and women how to live healthy lifestyles. She has taught a variety of classes including: Living with High Blood Pressure, Healthy Eating & Weight Loss, Smoking Cessation, and Managing Every Day Stress, always focusing on finding a healthy balance. Lisa welcomed the opportunity to impact lives in a practical way focusing on the whole person leading her into work as Support Group Facilitator for the Washington DC Welfare to Work Program, Program Coordinator for the U.S. Department of Health and Human Services, Office of Minority Health Resource Center and Manager of a Hospital Senior Wellness Program.

Despite fulfillment in her career, her personal life and marriage grew desolate. Shortly before her fifth wedding anniversary, she and her husband, Stuart, separated. In order to maintain her own health and well-being, Lisa had to practice what she had been teaching for over 10 years! The journey through seven years of separation and divorce served as her ultimate test. Having passed the test and remarrying Stuart (her same husband) a new passion for healthy marriages and families was ignited in Lisa.

Lisa has refocused her career from teaching about physical health to reviving the spirit of women giving them the skills and practical tools necessary to live healthy lifestyles as they care for their husbands, children, and communities. Today Lisa writes and speaks about love and marriage at local Churches and other women's groups. She also works as a personal life coach for married women. She and her husband Stuart celebrate over 20 years of marriage. They live in Washington, DC, and have three children. You can learn more about her work at **www.LisaEllisWilliams.com**.

What Other Women Have To Say

"I made a commitment before God to be my husband's help-meet. In order for me to be the best I can be in my ordained role, it requires intentional dedication to spiritual growth and development. Wife School study offers the opportunity for me to expand my understanding of God's will in marriage through organized and structured biblical application.

*Wives should read Wife School to strengthen their relationship with Christ, thereby increasing their capacity to be a more effective wife. Wife School will offer women biblical principles along with practical tools needed to enhance one's understanding of God's will for marriage." - **Kisha***

"I find Wife School to be a positive influence in my life. Lisa has established an environment in which women can encourage themselves and one another. She uses her testimony to inspire us to seek God, not only in our marriages, but in every aspect of their lives.

*Women should read "Wife School" to reap the same kind of benefits and to know that a network of women is here to support them in both the celebrations and challenges that marriage brings." - **Terralon***

*"Marriage is such an important calling and is the foundation of our society. When our marriages and families are strong we will all prosper. Wife School teaches solid biblical based principals that help foster strong marriages." -***Lynette**

"During the difficult times in my marriage, I found the advice given by society did not align with what I desired for my marriage. Lisa and her teaching were more aligned with what I believed a wife should be and what my marriage could be.

*Lisa has a way of really speaking from an unbiased point of view. She captures the biblical principles and articulates them so clearly. I believe she is also a voice for our husbands because she helps wives understand the needs and desires of men. She teaches without threatening or taking away the dignity, strength and purpose of a godly wife. Lisa's work is truly an awesome thing and Wife School will support wives in an incredible way." -***April**

You can read more at www.lisaelliswilliams.com

Acts 20:19-21 NIV

I served the Lord with great humility and with tears and in the midst of severe testing by the plots of my Jewish opponents. You know that I have not hesitated to preach anything that would be helpful to you but have taught you publicly and from house to house.

To contact the author, please write to:
www.lisaelliswilliams.com

Contents

Introduction

Many women are passionate about learning God's plan for marriage and want to develop into the virtuous wives they were created to be. If you are like the many wives who have come to this study looking for some change in their marriage, change in their husband, and some change in their circumstances, then you will leave this study knowing just how much God can make change happen for the woman who diligently seeks Him.

You will learn things you can do to grow in your position as wife and how to tackle the difficult parts of the job.

In "Wife School" you will be given practical strategies to keep love alive in your heart and win your husband without a word!

The Wife School curriculum is developed from Lisa's marriage testimony after surviving seven years of separation and divorce, culminating in victory through remarriage to the same husband. With her husband's inspiration and God leading, Lisa is bringing lessons she learned in wife school to you!

Taught in 3 classes you will:

- Learn to incorporate Biblical principles in your marriage and how to guard it from the outside world.
- Develop practical strategies for handling common marriage issues.
- Focus on personal growth and healthy living using prayer and devotion practices.
- Participate in Kingdom building by establishing godly friendships with wives who want to stay married, holding

one another accountable, and impacting your community through righteous living.

You will notice that this study uses the Bible as the primary reference. You should have one available for each class. Several versions are available but Lisa uses the New King James version as her primary reference. She also enjoys the New International Version another excellent translation of the Bible. You will also need something to write with to maximize use of this study.

Class structure for small groups

You can also use this study with a small group. Each class lesson is presented as an interactive workshop containing these basic elements: Prayer, Getting to Know You, Hot Topic, Make It Personal, Building Your Community.

Prayer- 15 minutes Every class opens with prayer. Personal prayer requests will be accepted at the end of each class for you to pray for one another.

Getting To Know You- 15 minutes Fun activity and conversation starter used to involve everyone in the group and to lay the foundation for the topic

Hot Topic- 60 minutes Here your Bible lesson is taught with enough time to include sharing and questions. You will use your workbook to follow along, answer related questions, and complete in class projects.

Make It Personal- 15 minutes This is time allotted for you to pray and meditate on the lesson. You will participate in guided journal exercises and create private entries that will serve as praise reports, testimonies, prayers, or take away-s from the lesson.

Building Community –15 minutes This is your time to socialize and actively build friendships with the ladies in your class. You will share life experiences, prayer concerns and laughter, and hold one another accountable for following God's word. You may also meet some new life time friends!

Lisa's Tips for Success in Wife School

- Decide-What's most important.
- Do- What's most important.
- Delete- What's most detrimental.

My class hostess is:

_____

Contact number is:

_____

Building Your Community

It is important to get to know the women in your class. Each wife brings her unique gifts and talents to the group. This is a wonderful opportunity to build friendships with like-minded women who desire to live in God-centered marriages, just like you!

Use the space provided to share contact information. You may also prefer to use your cell phone or other digital device. The goal is for you to find a way to connect outside of class. It is **NOT** recommended that you use social media to communicate with one another about topics or issues discussed in Wife School.

If you want to promote Wife School or the teaching of Lisa Ellis Williams, you can easily share pages from her blog, Facebook Speaker page or Twitter page by going to the website.

NAME	PHONE

Class One

Studying the Blueprint

Class One - Studying the Blue Print

ACTIVITY

You said YES! Take a moment to remember your engagement and your wedding.

Fill in the blanks below to help you.

Your Husband's Name: *William David John*

Your Wedding Date: *6 — 22 — 13*

What was the weather like?
Beautiful

How many guests witnessed your ceremony?
85

Describe your wedding dress?
Elegnat and perfect for me

How did wearing it make you feel? *Like a Queen*

What does your wedding ring look like? Is it gold, platinum, a band of diamonds? Do you have other stones? How big are the gems?

White Silver w/ several diamonds

Do you remember flashing it around when you first got it? Describe your husband's proposal:

Yes, I do. He went to Jared Christmas Eve - the box was in a day pair of snow boots.

Remember: You said YES.

Light Bulb Note:

My husband proposed to me in Hendersonville, TN @ my cousins/sister-in-law house w/out a ring! My entire family was there! What an awesome feeling that was!

Topic

On Becoming:

Your engagement time is worth remembering. This season was probably one of the most exciting times of your life and you may not have even realized how many of your thoughts were consumed with **becoming**.

The dictionary.com defines "become" as a verb meaning: to come, change or come to be. To be attractive on, to benefit on appearance, to be suitable or necessary to the dignity, situation, or responsibility of:

- You were becoming.
- You **became** his girlfriend. You **became** engaged.
- You **became** his fiancé. You **became** his wife.

Read and write **Genesis 2:18** *It's not good for man to be alone, I will make him a helper who is just right for him,*

Now you are trying to **become** the wife God created you to be. A virtuous wife!

The Blue Print:

Before any structure is built the architect creates a blue print. The blue print serves as a plan of action guiding the construction process and making sure the final structure actually resembles the original vision. For the sake of this study, God is our architect. Marriage was His vision and He built it according to a blueprint.

Read this practical view of the marriage blue print.

- God created man in his own image. Genesis 2:7 (NKJV) reads: And the LORD God formed man *of* the dust of the ground, and breathed into his nostrils the breath of life; and man became a living being.

- He decided that man shouldn't be alone so He had another god sized idea! Genesis 2:18 (NKJV) reads: And the LORD

God said, "*It is* not good that man should be alone; I will make him a helper comparable to him."

- You were made from the inner parts of your husband and then you were brought to your husband. You were given to him by God. Genesis 2: 21-22 (NKJV) reads: And the LORD God caused a deep sleep to fall on Adam, and he slept; and He took one of his ribs, and closed up the flesh in its place. [22] Then the rib which the LORD God had taken from man He made into a woman, and He brought her to the man.

- God married you and your husband. Your union foundation was laid according to the blue print. Genesis 2:24 reads: Therefore a man shall leave his father and mother and be joined to his wife, and they shall become one flesh.

- Your marriage is designed to be a reflection of the great mystery concerning Christ and the Church. We often hear about how God through the Son, Jesus Christ, loves His bride, the Church.

Read Ephesians 5: 22-32. Pray for understanding and a vision for how God views Jesus and His Church. Write your thoughts.

_____
_____
_____
_____
_____
_____
_____

Your role in the ultimate design:

According to Genesis 2:24, what did God's design look like? The architect of your marriage created a structure where:

- Your husband was to leave father and mother.
- Your husband was to be joined to you.
- You and your husband were to **become** one flesh.

The first 2 items have to do with your husband. These are areas you can pray about but, you cannot do anything about. Wisdom reminds wives, that you can neither control nor change your husband. You can and should pray for change in areas that you know he is weak.

Lisa's Tip for Success

- Accept your limitations.
- Only God can change your husband.

Many wives get hung up on what their husbands are "not" doing but, in Wife School you are focusing on you. Are you willing to let God change you? *YES!*

Activity:
Write a list of ways you have been trying to change your husband. Hint. Think of the things you have been praying for lately.

- *a closer relationship w/ God*
- *patience w/ me*
- *protection for Him / children*
- *good health*
- *to be the leader and that I follow (w/ God's help)*

11

_____

_____

_____

_____

Now that you have that out of your system, let's pay attention to the many ways God is growing and changing things in you!

Wife School helps you to adopt and live by 1 Peter 3:1-2 (NLT) which reads: In the same way, you wives must accept the authority of your husbands. Then, *even if some refuse to obey the Good News, your godly lives will speak to them without any words. They will be won over by observing your pure and reverent* lives. *(Emphasis mine)*

Good news. Wives you can win your husband by what you do!

Do what you can do

You are to work towards **becoming** one flesh. This goal involves learning to implement new ways of living and being willing to experience spiritual growth.

If you are thinking that you became one flesh on your wedding day. Go back and read the definition of **become**.

Becoming one flesh is a process and it does not happen overnight. You desire to become the godly wife you were meant to be because, the wife you are today doesn't feel complete. Your heart tells you that something is missing.

In this study you are discovering small but crucial missing pieces. So far you have learned that:

- Building your marriage is a process.
- Building a sound marriage structure must be done by God's original blueprint.
- Building your marriage is not under your total control.

Be Honest with yourself.
Is this really important to you, why or why not?

YES, it is! Because it's important to God and my gift from God (my husband) I deserve to be pleased. He's a good man, I don't want to disappoint God or Daniel.

Become One by:

I.   Working according to the timeline.

When seasons of marriage change and you find yourself in the "for worse" times it is hard to picture continuing in the marriage. Friends, family, even members of your Church may tell you to get out. Your husband may be asking to separate or you may have agreed to allow time for a "break." All of these things happen in real life marriages just like yours. It may have already happened to you.

Lisa's Success Tip:

Wives live **through** "for worse" seasons in their marriages.
When you find yourself at a crossroads, Stop! Wives who are striving for excellence learn to avoid making major decisions based

on heightened emotions.*(*This study is NOT advising you against seeking professional help when you deem it necessary for safety or any other reason.*)

Now decide to build your marriage according to the agreed upon timeline.

Here is a sample copy of the vows. Your legal vows may vary based on where you married. **Fill in the blanks below with examples of each line. Pay special attention to the timeline.**

I _Janene_ take

thee _David_ To be my wedded Husband,

To have: _because God blessed_ and _me w/ him_

To hold: _to hug / snuggle_ from _time to time._

This day forward _each day w/_ , _baby steps_

For better _to celebrate an_ _accomplishment each day,_

For worse _even when I feel_ _like I'm going backwards_

For richer _____

For poorer _When bills are funny_

In sickness _to exercise together_ and

In health _care for Him (as he_ _allows)_

To love _w/ patience / kindness_ and

To cherish *each day w/ him* _____ til

Death do us part *in our elderly age (in numbers,)*

Thereto I give my solemn promise.

Date ~~⊘⊘⊘⊘⊘⊘⊘~~ *6–22–13*

Today's date *4–5–17*

Did you ever stop to consider some of the circumstances life would include in your contract? Did you write any of these examples?

To have: To claim him as your own because, another woman may want him for herself.

To hold: To embrace him often taking time to notice his scent, changes in his skin, and sink into his arms.

This day forward: To get a fresh start every day.

For better: To celebrate times of peace, harmony, laughter, and giving.

For worse: To live through long periods of silence, selfishness, lack of attention, no affection, negative talk, boredom, loneliness, or more. (This list can be endless)

For richer: To pay bills on time, invest well, and live debt free.

For poorer: To accumulate more bills than you can pay, have no extra resources, fear losing your house, failed business, avoid collection calls, and feel like a slave to your lenders.

In sickness: To care for a cold, allergies, a heart attack, a stroke, or cancer.

In health: To enjoy regular exercise, healthy eating, low stress living, and fun.

To love: As defined in 1 Cor. 13: 4-8

To cherish: To place a high value on, hold close, and treat as fragile.

"Till death do us part" To admit that is a long time!

When in doubt remember, you said yes. Honor the timeline.

Your work as a wife is set for completion the day you die. Your promise was until death do you part.

Look up Proverbs 31:12 to fill in the blanks. The Bible states a wife of noble character does her husband good and not harm _____ the _____ of _____ _____.

You become one flesh as you work according to the life timeline.

II.   Working to honor your promise

Have you ever been instructed to "put God first in your marriage?" I remember this saying was inscribed in numerous cards I received on my wedding day. It seemed like an easy piece of advice to follow however there are seasons of life especially early in marriage when you spend so much time being concerned about the affairs of this world and living to please your husband that you push aside your focus on God.

Before you deny it, keep reading.
The Apostle Paul understood this when he wrote these words in 1Corinthians 7:33-35 NIV

[33] *But a married man is concerned about the affairs of this world—how he can please his wife—* [34] *and his interests are divided. An unmarried woman or virgin is concerned about the Lord's affairs: Her aim is to be devoted to the Lord in both body and spirit.* **But a married woman is concerned about the affairs of this world**—*how she can please her husband.* [35] *I am saying this for your own good, not to restrict you, but that you may live in a right way in undivided devotion to the Lord.* (Emphasis mine)

Name some of the affairs of this world that you are facing right now.

Lach of ttimacy w/ husband
- Concern for daughter / grandson God
in relationship w/ E
- Gun Violence
- getting older
_-_

Examine your daily schedule. Note even the smallest ways you have pushed God and your faith practices aside to deal with them?

Laziness - getting home after
work and not wanting to do
anything but get comfort food
and watch comforting movies.

Are there any ways that you put your husband before God? If so, note them here.

Nope. Nothing that I can
think of. I put my selfish
lazy ways before them.
Lord, please forgive me /
help me.

You become one with your husband by keeping your promise to God. Luke 10:27 (NIV) gives some guidance. "'Love the Lord your God with all your heart and with all your soul and with all your strength and with all your mind'; and, 'Love your neighbor as yourself.'"

Talk with a friend and identify ways to keep God a top priority in your everyday life so that your marriage can be influenced by your spiritual growth. Here are a few to get you started:

- Keep your devotion time every day.
- Attend a Bible teaching Church regularly.
- Use a journal to capture God's movement in your life.
- Refrain from making choices based on high emotion.
- Use girlfriends to remind you to read your Bible.
- Pray with a group.

the check marks are the ones that I need to do more of

Make It Personal:

1.) Memorize: Genesis 2:18.
And the Lord God said, "It is not good that man should be alone; I will make him a helper comparable to him." (NKJV)

2.) Are you in or out? Write a love letter to your husband restating your commitment to staying in your marriage until "death do you part." You do not have to share this letter. Read Proverbs 31:10-31 for help writing your letter.

Write your thoughts, notes, and prayers   4-5-1?

Honey, you deserve more than I'm giving you. So, please forgive me for allowing my lazy selfish flesh to hinder my closeness w/ you!

Lord, I need ur help to get back on track. I repent and ~~beg~~ acknowledge my selfishness, I can't get back w/out you!

Notes of Lessons Learned

Class Two

Your Home Based Ministry

Class Two - Your Home Based Ministry

ACTIVITY

Goal:

This activity is designed to help you see your physical surroundings through the eyes of God and to help you identify small changes you can make to build your home and marriage based on wisdom.

Draw a picture of your home in the space provided.

Write 10 statements that describe your home to someone who has never visited.

1. _____
   _____
2. _____
   _____
3. _____
   _____
4. _____
   _____
5. _____
   _____
6. _____
   _____
7. _____
   _____
8. _____
   _____
9. _____
   _____
10. _____
    _____

Write 3 statements that others use to describe your home once they visit.

1. _____

_____

2. _____

_____

3. _____

_____

Do you like your home?
Yes _____Not really_____

Do you have fun in your home?
Yes_____ Not really_____

Do you invite people into your home often?
Yes_____ Not really_____

Why or why not?

_____
_____
_____
_____
_____
_____
_____

Do you find peace in your home?
Yes_____ Not really_____

Was decorating your home a joint project for you and your husband? Yes_____ No_____

Is it clear to visitors that both you and your husband's personality are reflected in your home?

Yes_____ Not really_____

Lisa's Tip for Success:

- Be willing to accept that your home should be shared by you, your husband, and God.

Stop right now and pray!

Ask God to reveal the areas in your home that need to change in order for everyone to be represented.

Topic

Your Home Based Ministry:

The Bible tells us that with wisdom a women builds her home but, the opposite also holds true. A lack of wisdom or an increase in foolishness tears down her home.

Write Proverbs 14:1

_____

_____

_____

The wise woman builds her house, but the foolish pulls it down with her hands. (Proverbs 14:1 NKJV)

Take Action! Commit to finding wisdom and using it to build your home. Why?

Home is the marriage headquarters.

The dictionary.com defines "headquarters" as a noun meaning: 1.) center of operations from which orders are issued, the chief administrative office of an organization. 2.) the offices or working location of a military commander, the place from which the commander customarily issues orders. 3.) a military unit consisting of the commander, his staff, and other assistants.

As you grow closer to God and to your husband, you will begin to draw closer to home. You will use the activity of stepping back and glancing around your physical structure to periodically assess the amount of wisdom you are using to build your home atmosphere.

Your goal as a godly wife is to build, refresh, and renovate, not tear down your headquarters.

WARNING! This is not as easy as it appears. You will make mistakes and frequently forget about your goals. How do I know? Romans 3:10 reads "There is none righteous, no, not one" (NKJV). That includes you dear sister. Brace yourself! Building your marriage headquarters is a process.

When you go astray don't waste time feeling guilty. It is unproductive. Follow these 3 easy steps to get back on track.

1.) ADMIT that you are off course.

Write 1 John 1:9

_____

_____

_____

_____

If we confess our sins, He is faithful and just to forgive us our sins and to cleanse us from all unrighteousness. NKJV

2.) **RECOMMIT** *your home to God and focus once again on renovating His headquarters.*

Write Proverbs 16:3

_____

_____

_____

_____

_____

Commit your works to the LORD, and your thoughts will be established. NKJV

3.) **PROCEED** *full speed ahead by praying and working your plan.*

Write Psalm 33:11

_____

_____

_____

_____

_____

The counsel of the LORD stands forever, the plans of His heart to all generations. (NKJV)

In the Wife School study, the "Blue Print" you learned to view God as the architect of your marriage. The focus was largely internal as you cleared your mind and heart of the world's debris. You laid a solid foundation and now you are prepared to build on it.

In this lesson you will:

- Define your space
- Determine your priorities
- Define your boundaries

Godly wives, protect the place where God issues orders and instructions. A wise woman builds a home that reflects God's original vision for her marriage.

Define Your Space

Who is the headquarters built to serve? Go back and read the definition of headquarters to fill in the blanks below.

Who is in the headquarters?

1.)

_____

_____

2.)

_____

_____

3.)

_____

_____

Your home should always have spaces for these people.

1) Commander= God
2) His Staff= Husband and Wife

3) Other Assistants= Children and other dependents

Think back to the picture of your home. Who occupies most of the space? Many wives say they do. Others sadly admit that their children take up most of the room in their house. Still others report living in a "man's cave". Are you willing to admit that some places in your home seem to be held captive?

Consider the following scenarios:

A wife paints her bedroom pastel colors and decorates it using lace, flowers, ribbon and other dainty accents knowing that her husband does not like them. She regularly works from the room covering the bed with her lap top, books, and papers. His pillow is covered with her clothes. She wonders to herself why her husband never comes to bed until after she is asleep. She is also sad thinking that they are seldom intimate at night.

Who is this space created for?

_____
_____
_____

What renovations can she make to this room in her headquarters?

_____
_____
_____
_____
_____
_____

A wife and mother of young children, creates space in the house for them to play. She reads a lot of child rearing books and is careful to purchase toys that are both safe and educational. The young children have free reign at home but, their toys are found in every room in the house. Her husband repeatedly complains about tripping over toys and requests that they be stored in one designated space in the house. This wife questions why her husband prefers to eat dinner in the basement alone rather than with the family. She hesitates to tell him news of subsequent pregnancies praying Psalm 127:3 to remind herself that children are a heritage from the Lord.

Who is this headquarters created for?

_____

_____

_____

What renovations can she make to accommodate everyone?

_____

_____

_____

_____

_____

What spaces in your home have been claimed by only one person?

_____

_____

_____

_____

_____

Follow these guidelines to help build and renovate your marriage headquarters.

1.) Never assume that your home and marriage are in good shape. Survey your property using input from your husband.
Ask questions such as:

- Are you comfortable talking with me about problems in our relationship?
- Are there some decisions that we could have handled differently?
- Are your needs for dates with me, sex, and time for outside activities still the same and are they being met?

2.) When you notice a tear, peeling, or damage to your marriage contact THE expert for repair. Go straight to God. Do this immediately. Here's how:

- Pray no matter where you are or what you are doing. God will hear you.
- Be upfront with God and tell Him everything you are concerned about.
- Open your Bible and read verses that address your issue.

3.) Use top quality materials even if they cost more. Building costs may include but, are not limited to time, money, faith, and sacrificial love. **Be prepared to pay.**

- Pay with patience.
- Pay with endurance.
- Pay even when you don't see progress.
- Pay for the best books, devotionals, classes etc. to keep learning God's plan for marriage.

4.) Remember occasionally all marriages need upgrades. Keep your eyes and ears open to the Commander, so when he says it's building time... You can say "Yes, Sir! Let it be done to me according to your word!"

As you are building do not fear. Understand that you are a wise woman!

Lisa's Tips for Success:

- Create spaces where the entire family can relax
- Create spaces that are off limits to children
- Create a bedroom that is good for sleep and romance

Determine Your Priorities

What is important to you? When asked this question, do you become defensive and start to justify your choices about how you spend time and money? Do you have a standard list of things you value and repeat the list every time you are asked to consider your priorities?

Read:

Question: Is God really important to you?
Answer: YES!

Question: How much time do you spend with Him every day?
Answer: Well, I don't read my Bible every day. I know I don't pray like I should. I need to do better.

One common way to determine your priorities is to review your calendar and bank statement. Read the exchange again. Based on time spent, is God really a priority?

Yes _____ No _____

Why or why not?

_____
_____
_____

Lisa's tip for success:

Determine your top priorities using the "T.S.W." method.
- **T**hink about what matters most to you
- **S**peak your list aloud
- **W**rite the list

List your top 5 priorities.

1. _____
   _____
2. _____
   _____
3. _____
   _____
4. _____
   _____
5. _____
   _____

Look at your calendar and bank statement for the last month. Have you invested in your priorities enough so their importance is evident?

1) Yes_____ No_____
2) Yes_____ No_____
3) Yes_____ No_____
4) Yes_____ No_____
5) Yes_____ No_____

Write Proverbs 16:2

_____

_____

_____

_____

_____

_____

All a person's ways seem pure to them, but motives are weighed by the Lord. NKJV

Sometimes your actions do not reflect your top priorities. Your ways seem pure and your words sound good but, the Lord looks at your motives. Godly wives build their homes and marriages by regularly assessing their motives. Where do you invest time and money?

Where does your husband fall on your list? He should always be on your list.

By now you have placed him in the top 3 and your desire is to love, honor, and obey. After a while life gets hectic and you get distracted. Your "to do list" takes priority over him and you overextend yourself until anxiety and frustration set in. You get tired and frequently ask yourself how to get a break? You slow down and start cutting corners. The short end goes to your husband.

Beware of these and other ways your husband loses priority status in your life.

- You fix his dinner but, don't serve his plate.
- You welcome children home at the end of a day with a smile and open arms. When he arrives you can only give a polite hug and kiss that just missed his lips.
- You interrupt evening work for the children's bed time routine. You sigh when your husband interrupts you to share a new idea.
- You stop calling him during the day to say hello but will text him to make a stop at the store on his way home.
- You constantly complain about the household tasks he forgot to do.

Watch your time making sure that you spend it on your marriage.

Use these two highly effective methods to make changes when necessary

1. Remove an item from your list
2. Plan your time and invest money in what is on the list

Set Boundaries

Once you are clear about what is important to you, wisdom will help you protect it. Godly wives set boundaries around their homes and marriages. A boundary is simply something that indicates the region enclosed or the limits of your home and marriage. Everything beyond the limits stays on the outside. The boundaries you build will help ensure threats to your marriage remain on the outside.

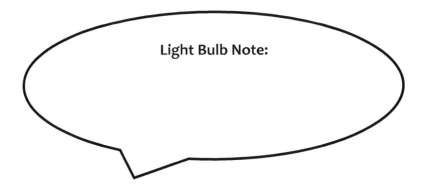

Light Bulb Note:

Discuss this list of things that should stay on the inside of a God centered marriage. Identify ways to build boundaries around each one.

- The ability to be yourself and live unashamed with your husband:

   Genesis 2:25 and they were both naked, the man and his wife, and were not ashamed. (NKJV).

   Where can you place boundaries?

   _____

   _____

   _____

- Having an undefiled marriage bed and producing children with your husband:

Genesis 4:1 Adam made love to his wife Eve and she became pregnant and gave birth to Cain. She said, "With the help of the LORD I have brought forth a man." (NIV)

Where can you place boundaries?

_____
_____
_____
_____
_____
_____

- Looking so beautiful to your husband that he compliments you:

Genesis 12:11 And it came to pass, when he was close to entering Egypt, that he said to Sarai his wife, "Indeed I know that you are a woman of beautiful countenance.(NKJV)

Where can you place boundaries?

_____
_____
_____
_____
_____
_____

- The confidence of your husband because he knows where you are when others ask him about you.

  Genesis 18:19 Then they said to him, "Where is Sarah your wife?" So he said, "Here, in the tent." (NKJV)

  Where can you place boundaries?

  _____
  _____
  _____
  _____
  _____
  _____

- Your husband's ability to protect you and your children from danger:

  Genesis 19:15 When the morning dawned, the angels urged Lot to hurry, saying, "Arise, take your wife and your two daughters who are here, lest you be consumed in the punishment of the city." (NKJV)

  Where can you place boundaries?

  _____
  _____
  _____
  _____
  _____
  _____
  _____

List other areas of your marriage that are worth protecting

_____

_____

_____

_____

_____

_____

Discussion Question: What are some boundaries you currently have in place to protect your marriage?

_____

_____

_____

_____

_____

_____

_____

_____

_____

_____

_____

_____

_____

_____

By setting healthy boundaries you will rebuild the deserted ruins of your marriages. Then you will be known as a rebuilder of marriages and a restorer of homes. (Adapted from Isaiah 58:12 NLT)

Commit to the LORD whatever you do, and he will establish your plans. Proverbs 16:3 (NIV)

Make It Personal

1.) Write Proverbs 14:1

_____
_____
_____
_____
_____

The wise woman builds her house, but the foolish pulls it down with her hands. Proverbs 14:1 (NKJV)

2.) Write Proverbs 24:3-4

_____
_____
_____
_____
_____

Through wisdom a house is built, and by understanding it is established; by knowledge the rooms are filled with all precious and pleasant riches. (NKJV)

3.) Your home is important and it should operate as your marriage headquarters. How you decorate it and use it matters. Hebrews 13:2 (NKJV) reads: Do not forget to entertain strangers, for by so doing some have unwittingly entertained angels.

Maximize the space you have.

How can your home be decorated to create spaces that reflect God, your husband, you and any children living with you? What renovations do you need to make in each room?

Outside of your home

_____
_____
_____
_____
_____

Living Room

_____
_____
_____
_____
_____

Dining Room

_____
_____
_____
_____
_____

Bedroom

_____
_____
_____
_____
_____

Kitchen

_____

_____

_____

_____

_____

Basement

_____

_____

_____

_____

_____

Other Rooms

_____

_____

_____

_____

_____

4.) List ways you can keep your husband and marriage at the top of your priority list.

_____

_____

_____

_____

_____

_____

_____

_____

Lisa's Success Tip:

- Ask your husband for his ideas

5.) Write a prayer asking God to help you:
1. decide what is most important,
2. do what is most important, and
3. delete what is most detrimental to your home and marriage

Write other ideas, notes, and prayers.
Remember to thank God for giving you a growing marriage.

_____
_____
_____
_____
_____
_____
_____
_____
_____
_____
_____
_____
_____
_____
_____
_____
_____
_____
_____
_____
_____

Notes of Lessons Learned

Class Three

The Art of

Being Right

The Art of Being Right

ACTIVITY

Read Proverbs 31:10-31(NLT) and discuss the questions.

A Wife of Noble Character

[10] Who can find a virtuous and capable wife?
She is more precious than rubies.
[11] Her husband can trust her, and she will greatly enrich his life.
[12] She brings him good not harm, all the days of her life.

[13] She finds wool and flax and busily spins it.
[14] She is like a merchant's ship, bringing her food from afar.
[15] She gets up before dawn to prepare breakfast for her household and plan the day's work for her servant girls.

[16] She goes to inspect a field and buys it;
with her earnings she plants a vineyard.
[17] She is energetic and strong, a hard worker.
[18] She makes sure her dealings are profitable;
her lamp burns late into the night.

[19] Her hands are busy spinning thread, her fingers twisting fiber.
[20] She extends a helping hand to the poor and opens her arms to the needy.
[21] She has no fear of winter for her household,
for everyone has warm clothes.

[22] She makes her own bedspreads.
She dresses in fine linen and purple gowns.

²³ Her husband is well known at the city gates,
where he sits with the other civic leaders.
²⁴ She makes belted linen garments and sashes to sell to the
merchants.

²⁵ She is clothed with strength and dignity,
and she laughs without fear of the future.
²⁶ When she speaks, her words are wise,
and she gives instructions with kindness.

²⁷ She carefully watches everything in her household and suffers
nothing from laziness.

²⁸ Her children stand and bless her. Her husband praises her:
²⁹ "There are many virtuous and capable women in the world,
but you surpass them all!"

³⁰ Charm is deceptive, and beauty does not last; but a woman
who fears the Lord will be greatly praised. ³¹ Reward her for all
she has done. Let her deeds publicly declare her praise.

1.) What things do you and this wife have in common?

_____

_____

_____

_____

_____

_____

2.) What areas of her life has she surrendered to God?

_____

_____

_____

_____

_____

_____

3.) How would you describe her attitude towards her life?

_____

_____

_____

_____

_____

4.) How does she show love to her husband?

_____

_____

_____

_____

_____

Topic

The Art of Being Right:

Don't you want to be right?

Dictionary.com defines right as an adjective meaning 1.) in accordance with what is good, proper, or just: (right conduct). 2.) In conformity with fact, reason, truth, or some standard or principle

3.) correct: correct in judgment, opinion, or action 4.) fitting or appropriate; suitable 5.) most convenient, desirable, or favorable.

By definition there is nothing wrong with being right so, as wives striving for excellence you want to master the art of being right in your marriage.

This lesson examines 3 areas wives can be right by living **RIGHT**.

- Right Standing
- Right Attitude
- Right Actions

Proverbs 31:10-31 describes God's view of an excellent wife. She has mastered the art of being right in God's sight and yet, visiting those passages can leave you feeling challenged on your very best day, overwhelmed many days, and plain defeated when you are at your weakest. In spite of how she makes you feel, there still remains a yearning to live by her example. She got it right. How can you?

The lesson begin as you read Colossians 3:12-15 (NKJV)

Therefore, as the elect of God, holy and beloved, put on tender mercies, kindness, humility, meekness, longsuffering; [13] bearing with one another, and forgiving one another, if anyone has a complaint against another; even as Christ forgave you, so you also must do. [14] But above all these things put on love, which is the bond of perfection.
[15] And let the peace of God rule in your hearts, to which also you were called in one body; and be thankful.

Who is verse 12 referring to? The _____
of God, _____and _____

Paul is speaking to you! You are the elect of God, holy and beloved.

RIGHT: STANDING

- Elect > Chosen of God
- Holy > Because God is holy
- Beloved > God's emotions towards you

Living right requires standing in the right position. How do wives remain in right standing with God? First you must remember that God placed you there. When the cares of life drag you down, exhaustion, stress, or health challenges prevent you from functioning at your best it is easy to forget that you are **the elect** of God and He chose you.

What does it mean to be chosen? The Greek word "eklektos" means select and implies favorite. You are God's elect, chosen, and favorite. Even when others criticize or reject you, God and your husband have chosen you. You are in right standing.

Do you remember a time when you felt rejected by others but your husband still chose you? Describe how his response made you feel?

_____

_____

_____

_____

_____

_____

_____

_____

Read John 15:16. How does knowing that you have been chosen make you feel?

_____

_____

_____

_____

_____

_____

_____

_____

Next you must accept the truth that God calls you **holy.** The Greek word here "hagios" means physically pure, morally blameless, or consecrated. God is speaking to those who are consecrated to Him. Leviticus 11:45 (NKJV) reads I am the LORD, who brought you up out of Egypt to be your God; therefore be holy, because I am holy. You are able to be holy because God is holy.

Read Psalm 32:1-5 and answer these questions: (*see make it personal)

Who is blessed?

_____

_____

_____

_____

_____

_____

_____

What were the results of keeping silent?

_____

_____

_____

_____

_____

_____

_____

What does the Psalmist tell you to do?

_____

_____

_____

_____

_____

_____

_____

What happened next?

_____

_____

_____

_____

_____

_____

Look up Ephesians 1:4. When did God decide that you would be holy?

Lisa's Tips for Success:

- Instead of pondering sinful thoughts, confess them.
- Reject lies that cause you to feel unworthy of God's call on your marriage
- Release Guilt and accept God's forgiveness.

Being right with God mandates that you be holy, you are holy because God is holy.

As if that was not enough, you are **beloved**. You are the elect of God, holy, and you are beloved. Beloved here is compared to the Greek word "phileo" meaning to be fond of, or have affection for, a personal attachment. This is yet one more way God feels about you.

Read Romans 8:38-39. How does God feel about you?

_____
_____
_____
_____
_____
_____
_____

[38] *For I am persuaded that neither death nor life, nor angels nor principalities nor powers, nor things present nor things to come,* [39] *nor height nor depth, nor any other created thing, shall be able to separate us from the love of God which is in Christ Jesus our Lord.*

Godly wives are his beloved!

Living in right standing allows you to start each new day feeling secure in God's affection towards you. He has a personal attachment to you. If you believe what God says about you, then what people say will not matter so much.

Considering your right standing with God (chosen, holy, and beloved), is there any area the Lord has pointed out to you during this lesson that you need to change?

_____
_____
_____
_____
_____
_____
_____
_____
_____

Write a short prayer to confess those areas right now and surrender afresh.

_____
_____
_____
_____
_____
_____

Right: Attitude
Once you are standing in the right position, your challenge is to maintain the right attitude. Let's explore what the right attitude is and how excellent wives maintain keep it?

According to Colossians 3:12b-13, what are the *right* attitudes?

1.)

_____

2.)

_____

3.)

_____

4.)

_____

5.)

_____

(Tender mercies, kindness, humility, meekness, long suffering)

How does the scripture tell you to access them?

_____
_____
_____
_____
_____
_____

To maintain the right attitudes, you must put them on.

Review the list of right attitudes again. Are there any that come easy for you?

_____

_____

_____

_____

_____

_____

_____

What makes the others more difficult to put on?

_____

_____

_____

_____

_____

_____

_____

Lisa's tip for success:

- Keep your heart tender towards your husband so it is easy to put on the right attitudes.

Get a partner and discuss various strategies to help you maintain the right attitudes in your marriage?

1.) Tender mercies- To have compassion, or pity with tenderness. Have you ever heard the saying, grace is getting what you don't deserve. Mercy is not getting what you do deserve?

How will you put on tender mercies?

_____
_____
_____
_____
_____
_____
_____

2.) Kindness- You offer kindness to other people throughout each day, make your husband one of them. How will you be nice and show kindness to your husband?

_____
_____
_____
_____
_____
_____

3.) Humility- Pride is the opposite of humility. Are there areas where you are prideful in your marriage? Do you have to lead from first place? Where can you put on humility instead?

_____
_____
_____
_____
_____
_____
_____

4.) Meekness- Exhibiting patience and living in submission exemplify this attitude. God calls the last to be first and tells wives to submit to their husbands in everything. How can meekness become a permanent attitude change for you?

_____

_____

_____

_____

_____

_____

_____

5.) Long suffering – Think quiet strength. Some things in life take time and don't feel good while you are living through the process of change. How will you embrace the attitude of long suffering and let God grow you into a more excellent wife?

_____

_____

_____

_____

_____

_____

_____

Note* this author is not instructing any wife to endure abuse of any kind or to remain in an abusive or dangerous situation. If you need help then seek help.

Excellent wives follow Paul's instruction and put on tender mercies, kindness, humility, meekness and longsuffering. Chose the right attitude every day of your marriage until "death do you part."

Read Colossians 3:12-17 from the Message Bible (MSG)

12-14 So, chosen by God for this new life of love, dress in the wardrobe God picked out for you: compassion, kindness, humility, quiet strength, discipline. Be even-tempered, content with second place, quick to forgive an offense. Forgive as quickly and completely as the Master forgave you. And regardless of what else you put on, wear love. It's your basic, all-purpose garment. Never be without it.

15-17 Let the peace of Christ keep you in tune with each other, in step with each other. None of this going off and doing your own thing. And cultivate thankfulness. Let the Word of Christ—the Message—have the run of the house. Give it plenty of room in your lives. Instruct and direct one another using good common sense. And sing; sing your hearts out to God! Let every detail in your lives—words, actions, whatever—be done in the name of the Master, Jesus, thanking God the Father every step of the way.

In addition to adopting the right attitudes, an excellent wife takes the right action. Regardless of anything else you can choose to LOVE at all times. Here are some actions that require faith.

Use Col. 3:12 to fill in the blanks and learn how to take the right actions.

Forgive as_____ and_____
_____as the Master forgave _____
Let the _____of Christ _____you in tune with
each _____thankfulness.
Let the Word of Christ have _____of the
_____Give it _____of room in
your _____
Sing your _____out to_____

Excellent wives allow the peace of God to rule in their hearts and in their marriages. You are called to peace. Begin each day thankful for your marriage and choose to live right in it. Now that you know the art to being right and have the tools, you can paint a right picture of marriage for others to admire.

Lisa's tips for success:

- Enjoy one another's company.
- Look for new strengths, and work through areas of weakness together.
- Don't let yourself get bored with being married.

Make It Personal

1.) Read John 15:15-17 (NKJV)

[15] No longer do I call you servants, for a servant does not know what his master is doing; but I have called you friends, for all things that I heard from My Father I have made known to you. [16] You did not choose Me, but I chose you and appointed you that you should go and bear fruit, and *that* your fruit should remain, that whatever you ask the Father in My name He may give you. [17] These things I command you, that you love one another.

How does it make you feel to be called?

_____

_____

_____

_____

_____

_____

Why were you chosen and appointed?

_____

_____

_____

_____

_____

_____

What fruit is your marriage producing? Read Galatians 5:22

_____

_____

_____

_____

_____

_____

Why is it important that your fruit remain?

_____

_____

_____

_____

_____

_____

2.) Meditate on Psalm 32:1-5 (NKJV)

Blessed is the one whose transgressions are forgiven, whose sins are covered. ²Blessed is the one whose sin the LORD does not count against them and in whose spirit is no deceit. When I kept silent, my bones wasted away through my groaning all day long. ⁴For day and night your hand was heavy on me; my strength was sapped as in the heat of summer. Then I acknowledged my sin to you and did not cover up my iniquity. I said, "I will confess my transgressions to the LORD." And you forgave the guilt of my sin.

Write a prayer of confession. Include the ways you are not living in according to your call to be holy.

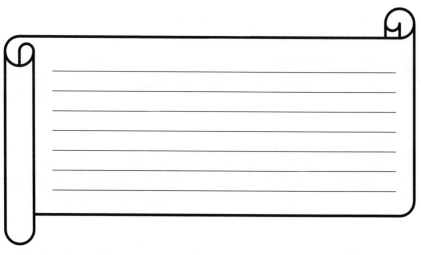

3.) Read Matthew 19:29-30 (NKJV)

[29] And everyone who has left houses or brothers or sisters or father or mother or wife or children or lands, for My name's sake, shall receive a hundredfold, and inherit eternal life. [30] But many *who are* first will be last, and the last first.

4.) Now read Ephesians 5:21-23. Write your reflections on these verses.

_____

_____

_____

_____

_____

_____

_____

5.) Take action and try these helpful tips to keep your marriage growing.

- Eat dinner together.
- Share your dreams.
- Read a novel and discuss it before going to bed.
- Learn to play a new sport together.
- Take a long drive with no set destination, blast music, and sing loudly.
- Visit a zoo and eat popsicles even in cold weather.
- Ride bikes in the park with or without children.
- Visit a museum, art show, or outdoor concert.
- Eat a picnic lunch during the work day.
- Watch the food network while preparing a meal together.
- Visit the sick or shut in together.
- Serve in a ministry at Church together.

You are married! Now is the **RIGHT** time to act like it.

Notes of Lessons Learned

Endnotes

Class #3

    1. James Strong, Strong's Exhaustive Concordance of the Bible: Updated and Expanded Edition (Peabody, Massachusetts: 2007).

Need More?

Is your marriage stuck in a rut? Do you ever wonder?

- When was the last time I felt happy with my husband?
- Is there more to my marriage than caring for children?
- What happened to the romance we used to share?

Do you ever feel empty, lonely, or angry at your husband for no apparent reason?

Do you love him but, can't figure out how to live happily with him? Or even worse!

Are you afraid that separation or divorce is knocking at your door?

What if I told you that fear of losing your marriage does **NOT** have control your thoughts!

- You can be coached to make positive changes in your marriage
- You can be taught to activate your faith and how to watch for God's answer to your prayers
- You can adopt the standard of living as a wife of excellence by doing it on purpose

I understand how you feel. That was me!

Over 20 years ago I married the man of my dreams and I was a good wife.

Then ...Everything Changed.

Life's demands were overwhelming, I had a baby, and I was tired all of the time.

I felt distance growing in my marriage. Other women seemed happy but, I couldn't figure out what I was doing wrong. I stopped investing in my husband. *I gave up and we split up.*

After 7 years of separation, we divorced...

Then...Everything Changed Again. I remarried my same husband and that is how I know I can help you.

You can learn from my mistakes as I coach you through life's changes and your marriage transitions.

Retain me as your coach and you will get:
- ✓ Free consultation
- ✓ Flexible telephone meeting schedule
- ✓ Unlimited text and email support while coaching
- ✓ Access to prayer support
- ✓ Designated 45 minute meetings to work on goals for your marriage
- ✓ Regular assessments of your progress
- ✓ Help to identify obstacles to change.
- ✓ Someone who has been there to guide you out

Get Coached Today. Inquire at www.LisaEllisWilliams.com

Made in the USA
Middletown, DE
21 October 2016